DAD JOKES FOR NEW DADS

START EARLY WITH 304 AWESOME (AWFUL) JOKES AND CHEESY PUNS

THOMAS J. PEROTTI

CONTENTS

INTRODUCTION

What is the best 'hood' in the ghetto? Fatherhood.

You might have heard a lot about this 'hood' before, but it's pretty much guaranteed nothing could prepare you for what lies ahead. Nonetheless, this book is written to give you an edge over other dads in the comedy department, at least. I've collected 304 of the funniest jokes I could think of and presented them to you in this handy list. Have fun with them and keep them close at hand in case you ever need help diffusing a tense situation or just to add some classic dad humor to your personality!

1

40 JOKES TO GET YOU STARTED

Q : What is the scariest threat to a matchstick?
A : "You're on your last strike!"

.... ❧ ....

Q : Your mom thought I should tell you a joke about planes.
A : But I thought it would go over your head.

.... ❧ ....

Q : Why do the ducks keep attacking our dog?
A : Because he's a pure bread!

.... ❧ ....

Q : Your mom threatened to leave me unless I stopped buying comic books.

A : She said she couldn't deal with my issues!

⌣

Q : Why do rockstars hate playing for ghosts?

A : Because they don't want to get boo'd.

⌣

Q : Where can you find the best winter clothes in the United States?

A : New Jersey!

⌣

Q : I failed a health and safety course yesterday. It asked me what steps to take in case of fire.

A : Apparently, "Quick Ones" wasn't the correct answer.

⌣

Q : What did Jay-Z call his wife before they got married?

A : "Feyonce."

Q : My wife threatened to leave because of my obsession with horoscopes.

A : It left our relationship in Pisces.

Q : I failed a test in high school because I couldn't think of two man-made structures for holding water.

A : When I told my father, he said, "well, damn!"

Q : My friend Jack is a vegetable-themed ventriloquist.

A : I didn't know this when I met him, so you can imagine my surprise when Jack made the beans talk.

Q : I used to keep a diary filled with fun facts.
A : I called it the Know-It Book.

············· ∽ ·············

Q : My wife says I always put my foot in my mouth around celebrities.
A : I told her it makes it easier to converse with all-stars.

············· ∽ ·············

Q : My wife gave me a German dog for Christmas.
A : I named him Jesus, for the Lord is my German Shepherd.

············· ∽ ·············

Q : How do fish always know how much they weigh?
A : Because they always have scales.

············· ∽ ·············

Q : What do you call a tired pea?
A : Sleep-pea.

Q : Why did the pop star overheat after her concert?

A : Because all her fans left.

⌣

Q : Where does a pirate get their hooks?

A : A second-hand store!

⌣

Q : What is the best hand to write with? Neither.

A : A pen works best.

⌣

Q : Over a hundred years ago, two brothers believed that humans could fly.

A : Many people doubted them, but you can clearly see they were Wright.

⌣

Q : I was very proud of my wife when she delivered her first baby.

A : She was nervous, but I knew she had it in her.

······················· ༼ঔ ·····················

Q : The judge gave my brother a life sentence.

A : Luckily, he doesn't know how to read.

······················· ༼ঔ ·····················

Q : My uncle used to have horses, but one night, the barn roof fell on them while they were sleeping.

A : I guess it was unstable.

······················· ༼ঔ ·····················

Q : My wife's favorite singer is Michael Jackson. She's always telling me to listen to his music, so I played one of his songs today.

A : It was Bad.

······················· ༼ঔ ·····················

Q : What is the best way to make your pants last?

A : Make your shirt first.

Q : I signed up for a marathon in 2019, but I didn't go.

A : I signed up again in 2020, still didn't go. Again in 2021… this is a running joke.

Q : I bought my wife new beads for her abacus for our anniversary.

A : She wasn't impressed, but it's the little things that count.

Q : To all the people who don't cover their mouths when they cough:

A : You make me sick!

Q : Just burned 2000 calories.

A : Note to self: Next time, do not leave the brownies on while you take your nap.

·········· 〰 ··········

Q : I got fired from the calendar factory today.

A : Apparently, the boss doesn't like it when you take a day off.

·········· 〰 ··········

Q : I'm donating dead batteries!

A : Don't worry, they're free of charge.

·········· 〰 ··········

Q : The machine at the coin factory stopped working today, and I don't know why.

A : It just doesn't make any cents.

·········· 〰 ··········

Q : How do you learn to drive a stick-shift?

A : I don't know, find a manual.

Q : What does an evil chicken lay?

A : Deviled eggs.

Q : Why did the golfer buy a second pocket for his pants?

A : In case he had a hole-in-one.

Q : Yesterday, I discovered that navy ships from Norway have barcodes.

A : Apparently, they have to Scandinavian.

Q : What happened to the Italian chef?

A : He pasta away.

Q : Wanna hear the joke about construction?

A : Never mind, I'm still working on it.

~

**Q : What happened to the frog who got a ticket
and didn't pay it?**

A : It got toad.

~

**Q : You should always wear glasses when solving a
maths problem.**

A : It helps with division.

~

2

39 JOKES THAT GUARANTEE AN EYE ROLL

Q : Why couldn't the sesame seed leave the casino?
A : Because he was on a roll.

.... 〜 ....

Q : What was the name of the 45th president of the dance club?
A : Donald Krump.

.... 〜 ....

Q : How do you feel?
A : With your skin.

.... 〜 ....

Q : What does a lion call his best friend?
A : His mane man.

- - - - - - - - - - - - - - - - - ~ - - - - - - - - - - - - - - - - -

Q : What do you call bedtime stories for horses?
A : Pony-tales.

- - - - - - - - - - - - - - - - - ~ - - - - - - - - - - - - - - - - -

Q : A wolf gets into an Uber.
A : The first thing the driver says is, "werewolf?"

- - - - - - - - - - - - - - - - - ~ - - - - - - - - - - - - - - - - -

Q : Did you hear about the stampede at the circus?
A : It was in tents.

- - - - - - - - - - - - - - - - - ~ - - - - - - - - - - - - - - - - -

Q : What do you say when somebody tries to steal your cheese?
A : Nacho Cheese!

- - - - - - - - - - - - - - - - - ~ - - - - - - - - - - - - - - - - -

Q : Where does Waldo go to find himself?
A : Therapy.

⸏⸎

Q : How does a hamburger introduce his girlfriend?
A : Meet Patty.

⸏⸎

Q : Did you know that the first French fries weren't even made in France?
A : They were made in grease.

⸏⸎

Q : I wasn't sure about my beard at first,
A : but it's growing on me.

⸏⸎

Q : I farted in my wallet.
A : Now I've got gas money.

Q : What do Mermaids wash their fins with?

A : The Tide.

Q : They called the police on a child who refused naptime.

A : He was in trouble for resisting a rest.

Q : How do you make antifreeze?

A : Take away her blanket.

Q : If you have cheese but no crackers, what are you?

A : Crack-A-Lacking.

Q : What is a magician's favorite dance move?

A : Abraca-dab-ra.

Q : How did Anakin know what gifts Obi-Wan was going to give him?

A : He felt his presence.

Q : What is the first thing Santa's little helpers learn in school?

A : The elf-abet.

Q : What is the warmest place in the house?

A : The corner. It's usually 90 degrees.

Q : Why was the rock upset?

A : He was taken for granite.

Q : Why did Santa's helper get depressed?

A : He had low elf-esteem.

--------------- ∾ ---------------

Q : Do you think lightning wears boxers or briefs?

A : Neither, it has thunderwear.

--------------- ∾ ---------------

Q : What do you get when you mix a Christmas tree with an iPhone?

A : A pine-apple.

--------------- ∾ ---------------

Q : What do you call an apple fart?

A : A fruity tooty.

--------------- ∾ ---------------

Q : Why did the needle go near the balloon?

A : He wanted to be a pop star.

Q : What does a French guy do in the bathroom?
A : Oui-oui.

················· ༄ ·················

Q : What do you call a Minecraft celebration?
A : A block party.

················· ༄ ·················

Q : What do you call a helpful lemon?
A : Lemon aid.

················· ༄ ·················

Q : Why did God create man before woman?
A : He didn't want any advice on how to do it.

················· ༄ ·················

Q : What did the plumber say to the singer?
A : Nice pipes.

Q : Did you know the average person cleans their bedding once a week?

A : But that is just a blanket statement.

⸙

Q : Whenever you feel lonely, you should buy some shares.

A : That way, you'll always have a bit of company.

⸙

Q : My favorite jokes are elevator jokes.

A : They work on so many levels.

⸙

Q : What is the most hard-working vehicle in the world?

A : A tank because it works tirelessly.

⸙

Q : What was James Bond's favorite childhood game?

A : I spy.

Q : **Rugby looks much easier than Football.**

A : All you have to do is try.

Q : **I used to run track and field when I was younger, but I gave up.**

A : There were just too many hurdles to face.

3

38 JOKES TO ANNOY YOUR BETTER HALF

Q : Why did the salad go to the studio?

A : To get some beets.

.... ⌣ ....

Q : What does the cucumber say to the squash at the dance club?

A : Let's turnip!

.... ⌣ ....

Q : People say the USA is the best nation in the world.

A : Personally, I say it's Donation.

Q : How did triceratops feel after his big workout?

A : He was dino-sore.

・・・・・・・・・・・・ ∽ ・・・・・・・・・・・・

Q : I almost got hit by a car,

A : but luckily it was a Dodge.

・・・・・・・・・・・・ ∽ ・・・・・・・・・・・・

Q : What is Batman's favorite drink?

A : Just-Ice.

・・・・・・・・・・・・ ∽ ・・・・・・・・・・・・

Q : I heard my wife saying one of her children will never grow up.

A : When I asked her who, she said, "My Husband."

・・・・・・・・・・・・ ∽ ・・・・・・・・・・・・

Q : Everybody knows where the Big Apple is.

A : But does anybody know where Mini-apol-is?

Q : What do you call a tiny mother?
A : A minimum!

⌣

Q : How does a pirate measure distance?
A : With Yaaaards.

⌣

Q : What do cows write on their protest signs?
A : We just want to be herd.

⌣

Q : I don't trust Edam cheese.
A : I feel like it's made backwards.

⌣

Q : Juan and Amal are twins. Her mother only keeps a picture of one of them in her wallet because if you've seen Juan,

A : you've seen Amal.

* * *

Q : I saw a microbiologist today.

A : He was much bigger than I expected.

* * *

Q : The CEO of IKEA was elected president in Sweden.

A : He should have his cabinet together by the end of the week.

* * *

Q : Never spell the word "part" backwards.

A : It's a trap!

* * *

Q : I can tolerate algebra, maybe even a little calculus...

A : but graphing is where I draw the line.

Q : My wife asked me today if I had seen the dog bowl.

A : I said no, I didn't know he could.

Q : My teenage son treats me like a god.

A : He acts like I don't exist until he wants something from me.

Q : What does Jeff Bezos do before he goes to bed?

A : He puts his pyjamazon.

Q : I'm pretty sure the hotel receptionist was

A : checking me out.

Q : My wife tripped and dropped the basket of clothes she had just ironed.

A : I watched it all unfold.

⌣

Q : I was drinking my milkshake on a cliff, and I had a thought.

A : "Wow, this is ledge 'n dairy."

⌣

Q : Geology rocks,

A : but geography is where it's at.

⌣

Q : Is it just me,

A : or are circles pointless?

⌣

Q : I got attacked by six dwarves last night.

A : Not happy.

· · · · · · · · · · · · · · · · ~ · · · · · · · · · · · · · · · · ·

Q : I threw an iPhone into a lake the other day.

A : It's still syncing.

· · · · · · · · · · · · · · · · ~ · · · · · · · · · · · · · · · · ·

Q : I got a universal remote for Christmas.

A : This changes everything.

· · · · · · · · · · · · · · · · ~ · · · · · · · · · · · · · · · · ·

Q : Nineteen had a fight with twenty.

A : Twenty-one.

· · · · · · · · · · · · · · · · ~ · · · · · · · · · · · · · · · · ·

Q : I once swallowed a book of synonyms.

A : It gave me thesaurus throat I've ever had.

· · · · · · · · · · · · · · · · ~ · · · · · · · · · · · · · · · · ·

Q : I never say curse words.

A : I swear.

~~~~~~~~~~ 〰 ~~~~~~~~~~

Q : The shovel was

A : a ground-breaking invention.

~~~~~~~~~~ 〰 ~~~~~~~~~~

Q : My girlfriend dated a clown right before she met me.

A : I've got some big shoes to fill.

~~~~~~~~~~ 〰 ~~~~~~~~~~

Q : Did you hear about the dog that ran ten miles to retrieve a stick?

A : That sounds a little far-fetched.

~~~~~~~~~~ 〰 ~~~~~~~~~~

Q : The only thing flat-earthers fear,

A : is sphere itself.

Q : I'm never again donating money to anyone collecting for a marathon.

A : They just take the money and run.

⸻ ∿ ⸻

Q : What did Bill Gates say to Melinda when they got divorced?

A : "You can have the house, but I'm keeping the Windows!"

⸻ ∿ ⸻

Q : My wife and I were really happy for twenty-five years of our lives...

A : and then we met.

⸻ ∿ ⸻

4

32 DRY JOKES

Q : I just ate a frozen apple.

A : It was hardcore.

⌣

Q : They just pick-pocketed the shortest person in the world!

A : How could anybody stoop so low?

⌣

Q : Whiteboards are

A : remarkable.

⌣

Q : I diagnosed a man with wrinkled clothes today.

A : He had an iron deficiency.

Q : Someone told me a story about screws, bolts, and nuts.

A : It was riveting.

Q : I was once attacked by a group of mimes.

A : They did unspeakable things to me.

Q : With great power comes

A : a huge electric bill.

Q : I just got a new job at a prison library.

A : It has prose and cons.

Q : People treat waitressing like a bad job,

A : but hey, it puts food on the table.

⌣

Q : My wife told me to stop doing my flamingo impression,

A : so I had to put my foot down.

⌣

Q : My wife forgot the code for her luggage. I figured it out.

A : You could say I busted the case wide open.

⌣

Q : It takes guts to be

A : an organ donor.

⌣

Q : What do you call friends you like to eat with?

A : Tastebuds.

⌣

Q : Some people think a boombox is old school.
A : I think it's just a stereotype.

⸻

Q : Why did the Dj go to the farmers' market?
A : To get some fresh beets.

⸻

Q : I just got my degree in skydiving,
A : but everybody else dropped out too early.

⸻

Q : Did you hear about the woman who gave birth on a staircase?
A : She had a stepchild.

⸻

Q : It's probably not safe for me to drive my car right now.
A : But hey, bad brakes have never stopped me before.

Q : **I broke my finger last week.**
A : On the other hand, I'm okay.

Q : **My wife asked me to choose between our relationship and my career as a reporter.**
A : Boy, do I have some news for her!

Q : **I didn't think chiropractors worked.**
A : But I stand corrected.

Q : **My wife is mad that I keep introducing her as**
A : "my former girlfriend."

Q : **Some alligators can grow up to 15 feet.**
A : Most only have 4, though.

Q : Spent $400 on a limo, but I didn't get a driver for it.

A : All that money and nothing to chauffeur it.

Q : How does Gordon Ramsay make his chicken?

A : He roasts it.

Q : In college, I was so broke I couldn't afford the electric bill.

A : Those were the darkest days of my life.

Q : Would anyone be interested in being my companion?

A : Asking for a friend.

Q : Unfortunately, my obese parrot just died.

A : It is, however, a huge weight off my shoulders.

⠀⠀⠀⠀⠀⠀⠀⠀⠀⠀⠀⠀⠀⠀∽

Q : I got my best friend a fridge for his birthday.

A : I can't wait to see his face light up when he opens it.

⠀⠀⠀⠀⠀⠀⠀⠀⠀⠀⠀⠀⠀⠀∽

Q : What do you call a bee from America?

A : A USBee.

⠀⠀⠀⠀⠀⠀⠀⠀⠀⠀⠀⠀⠀⠀∽

Q : Craigslist is useless.

A : I searched for a gas lighter and only got 13,267 matches.

⠀⠀⠀⠀⠀⠀⠀⠀⠀⠀⠀⠀⠀⠀∽

Q : What is the most draining job in the world?

A : Plumbing.

⠀⠀⠀⠀⠀⠀⠀⠀⠀⠀⠀⠀⠀⠀∽

5

39 CLASSIC DAD JOKES

Q : Two vegans got into an argument last night.
A : Thankfully there's no beef between them anymore.

Q : You can throw an envelope as hard as you want,
A : but it will still be stationery.

Q : I met a soldier who survived pepper spray and mustard gas once.
A : He was a seasoned veteran.

Q : My son told me he didn't understand cloning.

A : I told him that makes two of us.

⌣

Q : My wife just accused me of having zero empathy.

A : I have no idea why she might feel that way.

⌣

Q : I can hear music coming from the printer.

A : I think the printer's jamming again.

⌣

Q : My new puppy just graduated from college.

A : He has a pedigree.

⌣

Q : Why is it good luck to say "break a leg" to an actor?

A : Every play needs a cast.

⌣

Q : Do you know why aliens haven't visited us yet?

A : They checked our reviews, one star.

⌣

Q : If you clean a vacuum cleaner,

A : you become a vacuum cleaner.

⌣

Q : How do you split the ocean in two?

A : With a seasaw.

⌣

Q : People are usually shocked when they find out

A : I'm not a good electrician.

Q : Which country has the fastest-growing population?

A : Ireland, every day it's Dublin.

·········· ⌒ ··········

Q : In my twenties, I used to live on a houseboat and started seeing the girl next door.

A : Eventually, we drifted apart.

·········· ⌒ ··········

Q : I just saw a friend of mine sweep a girl off her feet.

A : He's quite an aggressive janitor.

·········· ⌒ ··········

Q : What happens if you throw a Finnish sailor overboard?

A : Helsinki.

·········· ⌒ ··········

Q : How did the crow manage to become a lawyer?

A : She passed the crowbar.

⌣

Q : Recently I bumped into the guy that sold me an antique globe.
A : It's a small world.

⌣

Q : My friend couldn't afford to pay his water bill,
A : so I sent him a "get well soon" card.

⌣

Q : I am terrified of elevators.
A : I'll have to take steps to avoid them.

⌣

Q : Someone asked me if I was Russian.
A : I said I'm not; I'm just taking my time.

⌣

Q : Hey man, do you want this pamphlet?
A : Brochure.

⌢

Q : What does a house wear?
A : Address.

⌢

Q : I just found out Canada isn't real.
A : Turns out it was all maple leaf.

⌢

Q : My massage therapist was fired.
A : Guess she rubbed too many people the wrong way.

⌢

Q : What do you call a person missing 75% of their spine?
A : A quarterback.

⌢

Q : My wife threatened to divorce me when I said I was going to give our daughter a silly name.

A : So, I called her Bluff.

⎯⎯⎯⎯⎯⎯ 〰 ⎯⎯⎯⎯⎯⎯

Q : What do you call a sick eagle?

A : An illegal.

⎯⎯⎯⎯⎯⎯ 〰 ⎯⎯⎯⎯⎯⎯

Q : Finally, my winter fat is gone!

A : Now I have spring rolls.

⎯⎯⎯⎯⎯⎯ 〰 ⎯⎯⎯⎯⎯⎯

Q : I saw male wigs on sale for one dollar.

A : It's a small price toupee.

⎯⎯⎯⎯⎯⎯ 〰 ⎯⎯⎯⎯⎯⎯

Q : Never marry a tennis player.

A : Love means nothing to them.

⎯⎯⎯⎯⎯⎯ 〰 ⎯⎯⎯⎯⎯⎯

Q : I quit my job as a personal trainer because I wasn't big enough.

A : Today I handed in my too-weak notice.

Q : Thank you, student loans, for getting me through college!

A : I don't think I can ever repay you.

Q : How do waves say goodbye to each other?

A : Sea you later!

Q : What has four wheels and flies?

A : A garbage truck.

Q : Why was the banjo so sad?

A : It was always getting picked on.

Q : What are the hottest buildings on Earth?
A : College campuses because they have the most degrees.

⸏

Q : Somebody robbed the Apple Store yesterday.
A : Luckily it was closed, so there were no iWitnesses.

⸏

Q : My daughter told me she's hungry.
A : Odd, I thought I named her Heather.

⸏

6

42 JOKES YOUR TEENS WILL HATE

Q : I was recently accused of being in denial.
A : But this is obviously impossible because I've never been to Egypt.

--------------- ⌣ ---------------

Q : My son asked me what procrastinate means.
A : I told him, "I'll tell you later."

--------------- ⌣ ---------------

Q : I hate funerals that start before noon.
A : I'm just not a mourning person.

--------------- ⌣ ---------------

Q : What did the sea say to the beach?

A : Nothing, it just waved.

❧

Q : I hate queuing for drinks except for punch.

A : There is no punchline.

❧

Q : What is the best way to eat honey?

A : With your bear hands.

❧

Q : Spilled my coffee beans on the stove.

A : Got roasted for it.

❧

Q : Why won't Americans eat snails?

A : Because they're not fast food.

❧

Q : I, for one,

A : like Roman numerals.

Q : Why are French omelets so small?

A : Because one egg is un oeuf.

Q : What music do wind turbines like?

A : Heard they are big metal fans.

Q : Regardless of the price,

A : Velcro is always a rip-off.

Q : Nobody knows why Notre Dame burst into flames...

A : but Quasimodo has a hunch.

Q : People say SpongeBob is the main character,

A : but I think Patrick is the star.

＊

Q : What happened when thirty was hungry?

A : Thirty-eight.

＊

Q : What is Spiderman called when he's run out of web while chasing bad guys?

A : Peter Parkour.

＊

Q : What do you call someone who delivers Indian food?

A : A currier.

＊

Q : What does the clock do when it's hungry?

A : Go back four seconds.

Q : We should have known communism wouldn't work!

A : There were so many red flags.

⁓

Q : Did you hear the joke about the broken pencil?

A : Never mind, it's pointless.

⁓

Q : Where does the king keep his armies?

A : Up his sleevies.

⁓

Q : What is the coolest letter in the alphabet?

A : B, it's right in the middle of AC.

⁓

Q : My cousin's math teacher called him average.

A : I think he's mean.

Q : It's not like I'm addicted to brake fluid.

A : I can stop at any time.

* * *

Q : Glass coffins are now a thing.

A : I wonder if they'll be popular. Remains to be seen.

* * *

Q : Saw a man standing with one leg at the ATM.

A : Confused, I asked him what he was doing. "Checking my balance," he said.

* * *

Q : Of all my body parts, my fingers are the most reliable.

A : I can always count on them.

* * *

Q : My grandpa used to tell me a scary story about fighting with bears.

A : I wanted to tell you, but my wife says it would be too grizzly.

Q : Do you wanna know why I take the lift alone?

A : Can't take the stares.

Q : I don't trust atoms.

A : They make up everything.

Q : Mountains aren't just funny.

A : They are hill areas.

Q : What is the best pan to make sushi in?

A : Japan.

Q : Nothing tops

A : a plain pizza.

⌒

Q : I'll never buy camo trousers.

A : I just don't see myself in them.

⌒

Q : Today I met Bruce Lee's vegetarian brother.

A : Brocko Lee.

⌒

Q : I had a joke about a boomerang, but I forgot it.

A : Wait, it just came back to me.

⌒

Q : My favorite job ever was at the shoe factory.

A : When I got fired, it really left me sole-less

⌒

Q : I let my wife color my tattoos when she's sad.

A : I'm her shoulder to crayon.

~

Q : What did one DNA cell ask the other?

A : Will these genes make my butt look big?

~

Q : What social media app would Thanos use?

A : Snapchat.

~

Q : I figured out why an electric car is so expensive.

A : They have to charge a lot.

~

Q : I heard ants are the only animals in the world immune to all viruses.

A : Well, termites too. They have anty bodies.

~

Q : What color is the wind?

A : Blew.

.... ⌣ ....

Q : What does a rusty can of rust remover smell like?

A : Irony.

.... ⌣ ....

Q : Not all maths puns are funny.

A : Just sum.

.... ⌣ ....

Q : **The average height of a dwarf is 4 feet.**

A : That's a little gnome fact.

Q : **Getting paid to sleep would be**

A : my dream job.

Q : **What is a song that costs 45 cents?**

A : A song by 50 Cent featuring Nickelback.

Q : **What has 4 letters, sometimes has 9 letters,**

A : but never has 5 letters.

Q : **When life gives you melons,**

A : you might be dyslexic.

Q : I know a lot of jokes about unemployed people,

A : but none of them work.

⌣

Q : This Halloween, I wanted to go dressed as a band-aid but decided against it.

A : It's hard to pull off.

⌣

Q : Yesterday I spotted an albino dalmatian.

A : It was the least I could do for him.

⌣

Q : What do you say to a British person who has just hurt themselves?

A : UK?

⌣

Q : How much room does fungus need to grow?

A : As mushroom as possible.

Q : My company weighs tiny objects.

A : It's a small-scale operation.

·················· ᑌᗡ ··················

Q : A man walks into his home to discover all his lamps have been stolen.

A : He was de-lighted.

·················· ᑌᗡ ··················

Q : English puns make me feel numb,

A : but math puns make me feel number.

·················· ᑌᗡ ··················

Q : I tried to come up with a joke about social distancing.

A : This is as close as I could get.

·················· ᑌᗡ ··················

Q : What is brown and sticky?

A : A stick.

·················· ᑌᗡ ··················

Q : Why can't the bike stand by itself?
A : It's two-tired.

.... ⌣ ....

Q : Can February March?
A : No, but April May.

.... ⌣ ....

Q : Is it safe to dive into a pool?
A : Deep ends.

.... ⌣ ....

Q : David lost his ID.
A : Guess we'll start calling him Dav now.

.... ⌣ ....

Q : How many bones does your hand have?
A : At least a handful of them.

.... ⌣ ....

Q : Why did the picture go to prison?

A : It was framed.

Q : Why do ducks make great detectives?

A : They always quack the case.

Q : I hate vacuum cleaners.

A : They just suck.

Q : How do trees get on Facebook?

A : They log on.

Q : Why can't T-Rex's clap their hands?

A : Because they're extinct.

Q : What does Santa say when he's homesick?
A : There's snow place like home.

Q : What is big, grey, and doesn't matter?
A : An irrelephant.

Q : What kind of doctor is Dr. Pepper?
A : A fizzician.

Q : What is Thanos' favourite cereal?
A : Rice krispies, he likes the snap crackle pop.

Q : I don't often tell dad jokes.
A : But when I do, he usually laughs.

Q : What do you call an old snowman?
A : Water.

.... 〰 ....

Q : What do you call a woman with two brains?
A : Pregnant.

.... 〰 ....

Q : Hey, you know what?
A : Never mind, you never met him.

.... 〰 ....

Q : Why shouldn't blind people skydive?
A : It scares the dog.

.... 〰 ....

Q : Did you hear about the angry pancake?
A : He flipped.

.... 〰 ....

Q : Due to quarantine,
A : I'll only be telling inside jokes.

Q : A blind person was eating seafood.
A : It didn't help much.

Q : If I were to describe myself in three words:
A : Not good at math.

Q : I found a pen that can write underwater.
A : It can write other words too.

Q : My son threw a carton of milk at me.
A : How dairy.

Q : What is blue and not heavy?

A : Light blue.

⌣

Q : Whatever you do, never read an email that warns you about reading maps backwards.

A : It's just spam.

⌣

Q : I proposed to my girlfriend at the gym, but she said no.

A : Safe to say we didn't work out.

⌣

30 HALF-DECENT JOKES

Q : Which is faster, hot, or cold?
A : Hot, because you catch a cold.

·············· ⌣ ··············

Q : My wife gave me an ultimatum. It was either her or my addiction to sweets.
A : The choice was a piece of cake.

·············· ⌣ ··············

Q : I had to fire the guy I hired to mow my lawn.
A : He just didn't cut it.

·············· ⌣ ··············

Q : When my wife found me playing with my son's model train set, I was so embarrassed I threw a blanket over it.

A : I think I managed to hide my tracks.

⌣

Q : The thief who stole my iPhone

A : should face time.

⌣

Q : The swordfish has no natural enemies except the penfish,

A : which is supposed to be mightier.

⌣

Q : My son may not be the best roofer in the world,

A : but he's up there.

⌣

Q : What do you call a woman who sets fire to all her bills?

A : Bernadette.

⌣

Q : I can't find my "Gone in 60 Seconds" DVD.

A : It was here a minute ago.

⌣

Q : My wife and I share the same sense of humor.

A : We must; she doesn't have one.

⌣

Q : I ate a kid's meal at McDonald's today.

A : His mom was furious.

⌣

Q : My wife's mad at me because she said I never buy her flowers.

A : I honestly didn't know she sold flowers.

Q : You've got to hand it to short people.

A : Because they can't reach it.

⠀⠀⠀⠀⠀⠀⠀⠀⠀⠀〰️

Q : I stayed up all night, wondering where the sun went.

A : And then it dawned on me.

⠀⠀⠀⠀⠀⠀⠀⠀⠀⠀〰️

Q : I went into a butcher's and said, "I'll have a pound of sausages." He said, "we only serve kilos."

A : I said, "Okay. I'll have a pound of kilos."

⠀⠀⠀⠀⠀⠀⠀⠀⠀⠀〰️

Q : Why does Peter Pan always fly?

A : Because he never lands.

⠀⠀⠀⠀⠀⠀⠀⠀⠀⠀〰️

Q : Where do cows go on a date?

A : The moo-vies.

························ ༽ ························

**Q : The interviewer asked me if I'd be a good
waiter.**

A : I replied, "Well, you could say I bring a lot to the
table."

························ ༽ ························

**Q : Why did the hipster burn his mouth drinking
coffee?**

A : Because he drank it before it was cool.

························ ༽ ························

**Q : What is the difference between a sock and a
camera?**

A : One takes five toes while the other takes photos.

························ ༽ ························

Q : What did the scientist say when he found two isotopes of helium?

A : HeHe.

································ ❧ ································

Q : To this day, the boy who took my lunch money at school still takes my money.

A : On the plus side, he makes excellent subway sandwiches.

································ ❧ ································

Q : I spent my day in a deep-water hole yesterday.

A : You could say it was a day well spent.

································ ❧ ································

Q : I tried to explain to my 4-year-old son that it is perfectly normal to wet your bed,

A : but he's still making fun of me.

································ ❧ ································

Q : I walked down a street where the houses were numbered 64K, 128K, 256K, 512K, and 1MB.

A : That was a trip down memory lane.

Q : My son asked me what inexplicable means.

A : I said it's hard to explain.

Q : A man with a stutter died in prison.

A : He never got to finish his sentence.

Q : Yesterday I saw a person without a body or a nose.

A : Police asked me what they looked like. I said, "nobody knows."

Q : I told my boss I needed a pay raise; three other companies were after me.

A : When he asked me which ones, I told him the electricity, the gas, and the water.

Q : I used to have a job collecting leaves.

A : I was really raking it in.

CONCLUSION

I hope you've enjoyed this collection of dry, corny, or otherwise pretty awesome (awful) dad jokes! Remember to spread the humor and, above all else, have fun with these jokes! Sprinkle your own unique flair into them! The dad may not make the jokes, but it's the jokes that make the dad.

Printed in Great Britain
by Amazon